Und
HIGH
WHO IS GOD AND WHY DOES HE CARE

MATTHEW DOBSON

⌁UNDERSTANDING THE HIGHER POWER⌁

ISBN-13: 978-1508434481

ISBN-10: 1508434484

All Scripture quotations in this book are taken from the King James Version, New International Version, and New Living Translation.

Cover art by Teresa Scott Dobson (author of the Fruit of the Spirit: Bible Study for Preteens and The Twelve Outlaws: Disciple Bible Study for Teens)

Editor: Nellie Dobson

Author email: rmdobson@liberty.edu or rundobsonrun@aol.com

CAMELLIA
HOUSE PUBLISHING

Published by Camellia House Publishing

Century, Florida

I dedicate this book to my Grandmother,

Addie (Janie) Lorraine Simmons.

She walked with God and considered Him her
best friend.

TABLE OF CONTENTS

"I also pray that you will understand the incredible greatness of God's power for us who believe him. This is the same mighty power that raised Christ from the dead and seated him in the place of honor at God's right hand in the heavenly realms. Now he is far above any ruler or authority or power or leader or anything else—not only in this world but also in the world to come"

Ephesians 1:19-21. (NLT)

INTRODUCTION

What would become of our faith in God, if there wasn't some small desire within us to yearn for a Higher Power, something greater than what we can find in this world? I believe with all my heart that God knows who I am and what I need. I also believe God knows you, loves you, and will take care of you. It's when God seems silent that we don't think He cares. Understanding God, as the Higher Power will help us to process our life on earth and ready us when time on earth is done. But again, how can a person have faith in God when they know very little about Him? Over and over Jesus urged his followers to seek God and to have faith in Him. However, there will always be questions concerning the ways of God. Jesus didn't encourage people to insist on final answers or demand absolute proof regarding the things that affect us. Rather, we find that Scripture tells us, "His grace is sufficient for us".

A person with a limited faith might not be satisfied with sufficiency. They might lose the desire to dig deeper and fail to totally surrender their life to God. But, it's the maturing Christian, and the one who doesn't lack faith that claims the promise of Jeremiah 33:3: "Ask me and I (God) will tell you remarkable secrets you do not know about". God reveals Himself to those who seek to know Him.

I believe that God is the only Higher Power for salvation. He reveals Himself in nature, networks of relationships, countless situations and circumstances where evil is vanquished and goodness triumphs. God is in the pain of growth, the seed of sorrow, the wind that blows through the trees. He's on top of mountains, in our train of thought, in a child's exuberant laugh, and in all the laws of fulfillment which bind all people and Heaven and earth together.

For a new return to God it'll require a genuine growth, and maturity on our part. For it to happen in our country we must give up our old ideas about economics, social order, and national power and sovereignty. A greater understanding of God should reflect America's democratic experience of freedom and culture. We need to see God as a Higher Power who desires our collaboration and who will look to us as His people; as partners in the development of a better world.

This is why a democratic society and freedom is practiced by the very people that God created. How can human beings feel emotionally partnered with a Higher Power if in their daily lives they are treated as servants, legal property, or menial?

A person free from the constraints of sin will

learn its dignified position as a necessary partner of God. If a nation or group of people advance into the technological age feeling helpless in the presence of poverty, disease, and autocracy they will soon bow their heads in resignation and give up on themselves and God. But if a true understanding of God is pursued, attained, and supported by earthly authorities, hope will once again "rule the day" in hearts and minds. But don't count on anything other than your own motivation to really pursue and understanding of who God is.

This book doesn't seek to put down the value of self-reliance, but it does picture ourselves as dependent on a Higher Power to achieve all that we were meant to accomplish as living human beings. It's time we bring our idea of God into harmony with the fresh realities of our life. One of the reasons why America hasn't seen a great spiritual revival in so long is that we have gained the wrong idea and attitude that God is not in tune with our contemporary life. We've tried too much to conquer social justice and left Him out of our vision. America has had the feeling that there's no limit to its conquest of nature.

Let me say that any civilization that ever makes a virtue out of individual initiative and outstrips God in its achievement; will build a culture that finds it increasingly difficult to submit to the idea of a Higher Power, much less understand it.

There's still a chance in the American way of life for the creation of a new idea of God. We know that God does not change; His Scripture tells us this. But the ideas of self-reliant social powers have changed in American thought. We mustn't abandon our self-wills, nor should we quit dreaming about better lives for ourselves. But we must birth a new confidence in God. This can begin when we have a better understanding of who God is. We need to think of ourselves as responsible co-workers with God. In our prayer life and our religious teaching and preaching we need to catch up spiritually with the realities of daily living. We must intentionally weave God's instructions into our daily walk. This happens as we let the Holy Spirit discern things for us rather than try to fix it ourselves.

We need to stop approaching God with feelings of hopelessness, but with confidence that as the Higher Power, He will help us. We will then find God not in defeat, but in victory over the things that so often trouble us. It's not about mystical surrender. It's through a practical moral activity.

Our culture with its spiritual lag, must seek to understand the Higher Power that we all yearn for. We will make great strides in our faith when we come to recognize that we human beings should never expect final knowledge about Divinity. Our minds are momentary sparks of light, like the flashes of a lightening bug on a summer's night. The fleeting illumination that comes to us will be just enough to help us understand a little bit more about our Heavenly Father. And help us to see in the darkness the wonderful things He wants us to achieve in our own lives. To understand God is to understand the plans He has for you. With that thought, let's start the incredible journey of understanding the Higher Power!

R. Matthew Dobson

10 January 2015

THIS IS GOD'S WORLD

The earth is the Lord's and everything in it. The world and all the people belong to Him. Psalm 24:1.

OBJECTIVES OF THIS CHAPTER:

- To be more responsive in praise to God for His creative powers.

- To look for things in our lives that try to push God out of the way.

- To look for ways in which we may have abused some of God's good gifts in nature.

- To help people live with the facts of the Bible in a world that seems to have made God unnecessary.

CENTRAL TRUTH

Christians need to declare in a scientifically-oriented world that God is still the provider of all that we have.

Have you ever taken a trip to the mountains? What do you think about when you scan a spectacular mountain view? Have you ever splashed around in the warm waters of a coastal beach? Maybe you've admired the beauty of a flower in a rose garden. Perhaps you've gazed at the moon on a star-lit night. Is there something about creation and nature that turns your mind to God?

The mountains, the beach, and the roses are a few of God's creative gifts to humankind. They are intended to tell us something about Him. He is the God of beauty and order. Many thoughts cross our minds when we experience these scenes. How did they all come to be? Our answer boils down to two choices: Chance or God?

The Bible says that God made everything and it all belongs to Him. Those that study nature come forth with amazing explanations of everyday things that many of us take for granted. Some people think since scientists have been able to learn more and more facts about nature, the need for God as an explanation for all things has been diminished. It's important we understand that no amount of technical understanding of nature's processes will remove the need to answer the question of origins.

"In the beginning God created the heavens and the earth. Then God said, Let us make human beings in our image, to be like us. They will reign over the fish in the sea, the birds in the sky, the livestock, all the wild animals on the earth, and the small animals that scurry along the ground. Then God looked over all He had made, and saw that it was very good! And evening passed and morning came, marking the sixth day." Genesis 1

The Bible doesn't give many scientific details about how the world and humans came to be. It gives basic facts on both and woven into these facts are what scientists have been able to discover through scientific pursuits. It's easy for a Christian to be drawn into arguments and debates with non-believers concerning science and the Bible. We have to be careful about attributing too much scientific data to the Bible. And of course, some scholars of science claim more for their data than the facts would allow. It's a fact that all can accept that no scientific discovery has proved the Bible to be in error. The Bible has stood the tests of time, even while new scientific discoveries replace previously held theories about nature.

In Genesis 1:1 we have a short statement that answers who created the physical world (God), when (in the beginning), and what (the heavens and the earth). Within these simple answers we have to fit all of our scientific data. It comes down to whether we agree or not that a personal God is the one who caused the world to come about. It's hard for some to accept the Bible's explanation because it requires more than scientific truth. It requires faith! Faith that God is in control and always has been.

QUESTIONS TO CONSIDER:

- **What recent science news seems to threaten the Bible's teaching?**

_____

_____

_____

_____

- **What cases in school have caused problems in trying to accept the Bible and science?**

_____

_____

_____

_____

- **How do discoveries in space affect people's attitudes about creation?**

_____

_____

_____

_____

Perhaps even more controversy has surrounded the origin of humans than the origin of the universe. The theory of evolution gets the most traction when it comes to the scientific explanation of where you came from. Christians should strive to bring all of God's truth into harmony, truth from Scripture and truth from scientific discovery. This is difficult for many people because science believes man evolved from lower forms of life, where as the Bible says that humankind was a special creation different from pre-existing forms.

It's easy to admit that humans and animals have some common traits and characteristics. But Genesis 1:26 asserts two important things: 1) Humans are made in God's image and likeness; 2) Humans have dominion over the rest of creation. The primary difference between humans and the animal world is spiritual, not physical. We are more than just a higher form of animal life. We enjoy a special relationship to God! "Image and Likeness" doesn't mean we look like God! This refers to the spirit inside us. This answers the Spiritual reality of God. You can have personal fellowship with your God. Nothing else in the entire created universe enjoys that privilege.

After God created the heavens, earth, humans, animals, and all other living things He said, "It was very good." While the effects of sin distorted what

God has made, the physical world and its matter are not evil. In humankind's perseverance, some of God's creation has been misused. We tend to put the blame in the wrong place. God's world is good, very good! You might argue and say, "No Way! The world is evil!" Jesus explained things perfectly when he said, "It's not what goes into your body that defiles you. You are defiled by what comes from your heart." Our sinful nature makes the world a bad place (evil thoughts, theft, murder, adultery, greed, wickedness, deceit, envy, slander, pride, and lust). God's world as He created it is good! We are the ones who taint it.

QUESTIONS TO CONSIDER:

- **How does the theory of evolution distort biblical truth?**

  _____

  _____

  _____

  _____

- **What do you feel about those who believe that evolution is the process God used to create humans?**

  _____

  _____

  _____

  _____

- **What about life after death, if humans are no more than an animal?**

_____

_____

_____

_____

The biblical view is that we are all living under the control of the one who made the world. "The earth is the Lord's and everything in it. The world and all its people belong to Him" (Psalm 24:1). God's ownership is based on His creation. He made it in the first place and institutes the process in which it operates today. Psalm 24:2 says, "He laid the earth's foundation on the seas and built it on the ocean depths." The land and the seas exist in productive relation to each other. The supreme fact of life is not what the earth is made of, but the fact that God made it and we owe our allegiance to Him.

You will find some modern-day philosophers argue that God started the world originally, but has allowed it to "free flow" and continue to evolve with no divine interference. This view sees God as the starter and not the sustainer. The Bible doesn't support this; rather it praises Him for its diversity. Psalm 104:24 says:

"O Lord, what a variety of things you have made! In wisdom you have made them all. The earth is full of your creatures."

Even more, creation is dependent upon God for its livelihood.

"They all depend on You to give them food as they need it. When you supply it, they gather it. You open your hand to feed them, and they are richly satisfied. But if you turn away their breath, they die and turn again to dust. When you give them your breath, life is created, and you renew the face of the earth" Psalm 104:27-30.

Animals, unlike their Christian owners, are not aware of their dependence upon God. Otherwise "Christian animals" would be walking to church every Sunday morning on their own looking for a dog biscuit or a kitty treat! From the outside we see that we must provide for our animals because God made us ruler over them (remember Genesis 1:26).

One of the things that we have learned as a result of ecology and our study of living things is God has balanced the scales of His creation. We often try to rearrange things for our own benefit, but the whole environment suffers when humankind struggles to make the necessary adjustments. Nothing exists in isolation. Somehow and in some way if you tamper with one thing, you're going to affect something else.

We must decide within ourselves to remain true to God and all that He trusts us to care for. Whether it's animals or the environment (nature); we must see these things as blessings to enjoy and thank Him for them.

I once carried a group of young boys (ages 7-13), along with some of their fathers on a camping trip into the woods. There were about 15 of us with tents and a roaring camp fire at the end of the day. As we set around the fire, feeling the warmth of its glow, we talked about the goodness of God and we each made commitments to follow Him in our life. Being in nature brings God's personal touch to your surroundings.

QUESTIONS TO CONSIDER:

- **What are some spiritual experiences you have had with nature?**

_____

_____

_____

_____

- **How could a camping trip or walk in the woods teach a spiritual truth?**

_____

_____

_____

_____

This is God's world and all created things are dependent on Him. You can be assured that God has not abandoned the universe and His Spirit is still at work. God has made provision in His world for every man, woman, child, and animal. And every generation of humankind and animals owes its existence to the Lord. Life, not death, rules in nature!

FOLLOW-UP

Many chapters in the Book of Psalms refer to the animal kingdom. Be creative and compose a Psalm based on modern technology, instead of things like fish and animals mentioned in the Bible. What do you find in your world, school, home, and job that remind you of God? Start by saying, "O Lord, how diverse are Your Works!" Then go on to list His works as you observe them in the things you see.

OUR REBELLION AGAINST GOD

"For my people have done two evil things: They have abandoned me; the fountain of living water. And they have dug for themselves cracked cisterns that can hold no water at all" Jeremiah 2:13.

OBJECTIVES OF THIS CHAPTER

- To understand the root cause of sin.

- To examine a person's outward profession that rids them of their lack of commitment to Christ.

- To ask if God is really in control of our lives.

- To check against complacency and lack of proper reverence toward God.

CENTRAL TRUTH

A privileged position before God is no guarantee against personal spiritual breakdowns.

A Christian is always pressed into trusting God despite changing circumstances in their personal life. As far back as the Old Testament, outward professions of faith in God were tested by attacks of foreign armies and foreign gods. We live in a day when an outward profession of faith is a call for criticism and judgment by those who don't like us. It's easy to go to church and be nice when there's no sacrifice or inconvenience. But God will not allow such comfortable religion to exist without allowing our faith to be tested.

There's no guarantee we will have success in all the things we desire to do. And in the meantime, we all find our faith being tested. We must ask ourselves what it is we trust to give us happiness, security, and satisfaction in life.

External props of money, things, entertainment, sports, jobs, home, recreation, technology are sought out for the achievement of true happiness. The Christian must face each of these with the task of keeping them all in perspective. Christians commit themselves to the proposition that doing the will of God is a person's highest duty and their supreme happiness.

Society tries to navigate our commitment to God whether it's intentional or unintentional. Such were the conditions in the days of the prophet Jeremiah. The outward professions were there, but the people of God had slipped into a comfortable complacent kind of religion. They didn't turn their back on God, but there was certainly a lack of concern for holiness and godly living.

"Listen, you foolish and senseless people, with eyes that do not see and ears that do not hear. Have you no respect for me? Why don't you tremble (fear) in my presence? My people have stubborn and rebellious hearts. They have turned away and abandoned me. They do not say from the heart, let us live in awe of the Lord our God. Your wickedness has deprived you of wonderful blessings. Should I not punish them (the wicked) for this? says the Lord. What will you do when the end comes?"
Jeremiah 5:21-31.

The message and description of the culture of that day could be likened to our present times. We know what we should do, but the attraction of the world tempts us to try and see if we can have it both ways. The signs reveal that there's a tragic lack of true inner godliness.

QUESTIONS TO CONSIDER

- Is going to church popular in your community? Why or why not?

_____

_____

_____

_____

- Do you see outward evidence of religion with true godly living in your community?

_____

_____

_____

_____

- Is your Christian activity a matter of doing what's expected, the respectable thing or is it the result of a life-changing relationship to Jesus Christ?

_____

_____

_____

_____

Jeremiah called them "foolish and senseless people". What made their condition so bad? It wasn't ignorance. Neither is it that for us. It's the willful rejection of the truth. God and His commandments have been passed down from generation to generation, from parents to their children.

25

The provision of God is so that we would know the way to love and obey Him. The Bible says, "You foolish and senseless people, with eyes that do not see and ears that do not hear!" We have every spiritual tool at our disposal for spiritual discernment and to know how to follow God. What has happened is our spirituality has been watered down or crowded out by society's multi-faceted lines of communication and busyness. Our nation is guilty of giving God tokens of our time and attention. We think a Sunday School lesson or one preaching service per week is all we need to give Him. God deserves more than this! Much more!

Perhaps nothing is more tragic about people's spiritual condition than their blindness and deafness to the reality of a Higher Power. Because a person doesn't see and hear spiritually, they wind up in a "foolish and senseless" condition. You mustn't fall in the so-called "heathen darkness", rather step out into the light so that all can see that Christ lives in you. There are many people who have spiritual knowledge, yet they can't grasp the spiritual implications. It's not that people are stupid; they're just willfully disobedient and choose to do their own thing.

A problem that exist today is that the internet, books, and articles by religious leaders tend to be accepted as truth by the public simply because the author or speaker has a claim as to religious knowledge and has religious authority by virtue of their position. This can be a dangerous assumption. A person can be religiously informed and be a great preacher, but still miss spiritual truth. Spiritual truth made alive in you is dependent upon whether we intend to do God's will (John 7:17). With Christ, there's no separation between knowing truth intellectually and living the truth in one's life.

QUESTIONS TO CONSIDER

- How can a person check themselves to find out if their spiritual eyes and ears are working?

_____

_____

_____

_____

- What can you do to open your spiritual eyes and unplug your spiritual ears?

_____

_____

_____

_____

- What things in your life tend to produce spiritual blindness and deafness? What can you do about them?

_____

_____

_____

_____

Rather than go through life ignoring God, practice the words of Hebrews 12:28:

"We are receiving a Kingdom that is unshakable, let us be thankful and please God by worshipping Him with holy fear and awe."

Above all, let your love for God overwhelm all that you think, say, and do. Allow the broken parts of your life be put together by God's handiwork.

QUESTIONS TO CONSIDER

- **Do you think some people are scared into becoming Christians?**

_____

_____

_____

_____

- **In speaking to non-Christians how can you maintain the proper biblical balance between fear and love?**

_____

_____

_____

_____

In Jeremiah's day the spiritual diagnosis of God's people is that the "fear of God" was lacking and the people were deliberately violating God's will. The essence of all sin is rebellion. Every single act that you commit on you own has a corresponding root in a heart that stubbornly resists yielding to God. The central issue for everyone is what is my heart like toward God?

Scripture reminds us that "Like sheep that have gone astray, we have left God's paths to follow our own" (Isaiah 53:6). We make choices everyday that either honor God or dishonor Him. Sin is not only violating what we know to be right, it's also choosing the wrong path and straying into a state of being lost. Every person, great and small has to make a choice.

"There is a path before each person that seems right, but it ends in death" Proverbs 14:12.

There came a time in my life when I had to choose to live according to what my parents taught me or live my life based on what I personally thought was the right thing to do. Not that I intentionally wanted to rebel against my parents, but because I had to make decisions based on my own beliefs. I discovered that the right standards of behavior are learned and practiced by taking heed according to God's Word. If a person will simply seek God with their whole heart and know how much He loves them they can be saved from wandering and waywardness.

QUESTIONS TO CONSIDER

- **What dangers does a person open themselves to when they choose their own way?**

_____

_____

_____

_____

- **Will following God's way produce a better life for a person?**

_____

_____

_____

_____

- **How can you show a person, when faced with a choice, that God's way will be better for them than anything they can choose for themselves?**

_____

_____

_____

_____

The times I feel closest to God are the times I'm out in nature and experiencing the fresh air that surrounds me in the solitude of a forest or woodland area. Listening to the birds chirp or hearing the water flow through a rocky creek bed evokes peace within my spirit!

One of the aspects of fearing God is to acknowledge that the gifts of nature come from Him. Beware of spiritual rebellion for it produces insensitivity to even the common blessings of life. Don't ever take the small things for granted. The life of faith is a belief in God's provision for the necessities of life. To counter-act the affects of society's rebellious nature, Christians need to proclaim recognition of God's faithfulness.

QUESTIONS TO CONSIDER

- **Do you think the advancement of scientific technology has brought a greater or a lesser acknowledgment of God?**

_____

_____

_____

_____

- **How can Christian families avoid the pitfall of taking God's gifts for granted?**

_____

_____

_____

_____

Let's think for a moment if God didn't punish sin. What's the alternative to this? Most people have built inside of them a sense of seeing wrong-doing punished. What kind of society would we have if there were no consequences for wrong-doing? Our moral codes and "Halls of Justice" hangs together on the promise that wrong-doing is subject to punishment. Shouldn't we allow God the same prerogative? Abraham asked the question:

"Should not the Judge of all the earth do what is right?"
Genesis 18:25

God will always do right because He is faithful and just. Our sin and human rebellion is affront to God's holiness. Sin breaks the law and hurts the person of God. So, you can be assured the guilty will be punished in due time. For anyone that chooses a lifetime of rebellion and rejection of God's love, eternal separation from God in hell awaits them. The simple solution that can avoid this bad end is found in the following verse:

"If we confess our sins to him, He is faithful and just to forgive us our sins and to cleanse us from all wickedness" 1 John 1:9.

FOLLOW-UP

Suffering because of sin is a true picture of humankind apart from God. This is a true picture of the ravages of sin that will come to all generations.

We see the effects of rebellion in both personal and social disorder. All of the evils that take place in our world spring from humankind's rejection of God and their refusal to submit to God's way. God's view of sin is that it must be judged. The wonderful caveat is that God's forgiveness is available. At any moment we can escape the punishment by genuinely confessing our wrongs and trusting God to lead us into life everlasting here on earth and in Heaven!

GOD'S CONCERN FOR ME

"You are my sheep, the sheep of my pasture, and I am your God, says the Lord God" Ezekiel 34:31.

Objectives of the Chapter

- To overcome discouragement from adversity.

- To learn about God's promises for His forsaken people.

- To find safety and security by coming to know Jesus Christ.

- To understand consequences for wrong-doing.

- To appreciate the rewards from having been persecuted.

- To realize Jesus looks for, rescues, and cares for those in need.

Central Truth

Even though it appears God doesn't care, He is an unseen shepherd that's always at work frustrating those who make it hard on Christians and caring for everyone who sincerely loves Him.

One afternoon on a beautiful fall day I was running on a dirt trail not far from my home. As I got closer to the creek that runs across the road, I noticed what seemed to be a cat sleeping. As I approached it I discovered it was a cat for sure, but it wasn't sleeping; it was dead. As a sad sentiment came over me, three little kittens ran out from a nearby bush. It was clear that these feline friends had been abandoned and the "momma cat" could no longer care for them. I have a soft spot for forsaken animals and I wanted to do something. I ran home as fast as I could, found an empty box, and raced back in my car to the spot of the forsaken cats. I drove them to the local veterinarian and left the rescued kittens in their care. This was the best I could do for a few kittens that had no one else to turn to.

In the Old Testament, God's children often were forsaken by those who should have taken care of them. In the New Testament, Christ tenderly extended his love to those who were forsaken by society as a whole: the lepers, the poor, the sick, even the prostitutes.

One of the modern tragedies of our culture is that so many people feel lonely and cut off. We provide homes for the elderly and for abandoned children, but institutions such as these rarely provide the kind of love and care that people need emotionally and spiritually. The welfare system can help keep a roof over people's heads and clothes on their backs, but the basic needs of the human spirit can't be met with money.

Often overlooked when trying to meet the needs of people emotionally and physically, is the need to provide spiritual sustenance. The human spirit in combination with the Higher Power can accomplish great things even when the prospects look bleak. Society has a spiritual void that can only be met by God. When a person feels forsaken by God, loss of hope is the tempting thought for nothing else can permanently sustain other than God.

I've worked in various service-oriented institutions and organizations for many years and have found that institutional programs are not enough. People need to be reassured that God absolutely cares for them, no matter how hard their lot in life may be. Despite the liberal progressive thought, the government can't really instill this kind of hope.

Christians can and should be promoting the hope that comes from the Higher Power. But many Christians lose sight of the fact that the cast-offs of society also need the "Bread of Life" which is Jesus Christ. God cares, but most people won't be aware that He does, unless one of God's children takes the time and effort to show it.

In the first twenty-four chapters of the Old Testament Book of Ezekiel the main theme is judgment and moral necessity. In chapter thirty-four we see God's plan to restore His people. Without getting into too much contextual history we can see this restoration has some short-range and long-range aspects. The ultimate restoration of Israel and rescue of all God's children awaits the second coming of Jesus Christ! And this second coming will not allow Christ to be subject to human wickedness, but instead will judge it.

"Then this message came to me from the Lord: Son of man, prophesy against the shepherds, the leaders of Israel. Give them this message from the Sovereign Lord: What sorrow awaits you shepherds who feed yourselves instead of your flocks. Shouldn't shepherds feed their sheep?" Ezekiel 34:1-2.

The summary of what God tells Ezekiel is the charge that the leaders of the nation had been putting their own welfare ahead of the welfare of the people. The common ordinary citizen had suffered most. There was no recourse when their rights were violated. They we're getting left-overs from the leaders. God asks: "Should not shepherds feed the sheep?" The answer is obvious! The leaders knew what their responsibility was. The problem was personal greed was stronger than a sense of righteousness and justice.

Jesus echoed this same principle in the New Testament when he spoke to the apostle Peter in John 21. He said:

When they had finished eating, Jesus said to Simon Peter, "Simon son of John, do you love me more than these?" "Yes, Lord," he said, "you know that I love you." Jesus said, "Feed my lambs." Again Jesus said, "Simon son of John, do you love me?" He answered, "Yes, Lord, you know that I love you." Jesus said, "Take care of my sheep." The third time he said to him, "Simon son of John, do you love me?" Peter was hurt because Jesus asked him the third time, "Do you love me?" He said, "Lord, you know all things; you know that I love you." Jesus said, "Feed my sheep." John 21: 15-17.

QUESTIONS TO CONSIDER

- **Think of some modern examples where corrupt leadership has brought suffering to people. What is the Christian's responsibility in such cases?**

_____

_____

_____

_____

- Think of some cases where political goals have been put ahead of the welfare of the people.

- How can a Christian apply God's standards of righteousness to his or her political views?

_____

_____

_____

_____

- How might Christians pray for legislators, executives, judges, and law enforcement personnel?

_____

_____

_____

_____

In Ezekiel 34:8 God gave Ezekiel four reasons why He was going to act against the shepherds. The first two have to do with the condition of the sheep. "My sheep have become prey and are food for wild animals" God likened the physical suffering of the people to helpless animals before a wolf or lion. Their homes were destroyed, their vineyards ruined, and their families separated.

The third and fourth reasons concerned the shepherds. They didn't search for the sheep, and they fed themselves instead of the sheep. The leaders of a nation have a responsibility to care for the welfare of its citizens. No country should exist simply to satisfy the personal desires of its rulers. In times past we can see how many rulers simply exploited the country's people and its resources for personal gain. God says this is wrong!

The shepherds of Israel were supposed to be set apart; not prone to the temptation of personal power and ruthless exploitation. They were motivated toward wrong goals, so they made wrong decisions and the people paid the price for their stupid decisions. In modern times, spiritual hardness caused by political correctness and political foolishness is as strong as it's ever been.

Spiritual blindness is to blame for wrong moves and wrong decisions made by supposedly intelligent men and women who have political power. Spiritually blind leaders can often undo correct decisions and policies. People are then left to wonder if anybody cares about what's wholesome and good for the majority.

The leaders of any country, including ours, can and do make wrong decisions. Many times they "Have fed themselves, and haven't fed My sheep". From God's standpoint, both shepherds and sheep belong to Him. The leaders are accountable to God for the way they take care of the people. He allowed them to be put in charge and expects them to rule according to fairness and the laws of righteousness.

What's a person to do in the case of a shepherd or leader who abuses his or her power? It's interesting that God is motivated both by the suffering of His people and the guilt of His shepherds. Both are intolerable to Him. God says:

"I now consider these shepherds my enemies, and I will hold them responsible for what has happened to my flock. I will take away their right to feed the flock, and I'll stop them from feeding themselves. I will rescue my flock from their mouths; the sheep will no longer be their prey" Ezekiel 34:10.

God will not fail to care for His people as long as they obey and seek Him. No one can mock the laws of God without incurring the consequences of God's righteous displeasure.

QUESTIONS TO CONSIDER

- **What are some cases where Christians especially have been ill-treated by ungodly rulers?**

  _____

  _____

  _____

  _____

- **Perhaps there are some who feel they're being exploited economically and they're not being paid a fair wage. How can a Christian see God's** care in a situation like that?

_____

_____

_____

_____

- If you have oversight of people where you
  work, or if people are financially dependent on
  you, or if you rent property, or make loans to
  people, how does this passage (Ezekiel 34:7-10)
  relate to your responsibilities to the people and
  to God?

_____

_____

_____

_____

The love and mercy of God is never more beautifully illustrated than in Ezekiel 34:11-16:

*"For this is what the Sovereign LORD says: I myself will
search and find my sheep. I will be like a shepherd looking for his scattered flock. I will find my sheep and rescue
them from all the places where they were scattered on
that dark and cloudy day. I will bring them back home to
their own land of Israel from among the peoples and nations. I will feed them on the mountains of Israel and by
the rivers and in all the places where people live. Yes, I
will give them good pastureland on the high hills of Israel. There they will lie down in pleasant places and feed in
the lush pastures of the hills. I myself will tend my sheep
and give them a place to lie down in peace, says the Sov-*

ereign LORD. I will search for my lost ones who strayed
away, and I will bring them safely home again. I will
bandage the injured and strengthen the weak. But I will
destroy those who are fat and powerful. I will feed them,
yes—feed them justice!

The troubles of God's people are compared to "clouds and darkness". The sheep think they're alone, lost, and beyond help. Have you ever felt this way? So it is when the clouds of adversity surround us and overwhelm us. Out there in the unknown, God our shepherd is looking for us. The Higher Power longs to be found by us. He isn't waiting for us to stumble home in the darkness. He's engaged and actively searching for us. Most sheep don't have enough sense to start for home. Many times we too find it hard to make our way through the darkness. And some Christians keep straying farther and farther away. But God never stops loving us.

God says He will "Rescue us", "Bring them out", "Gather them from", and "Bring them into". We are God's sheep and He's our Shepherd. His promise is to search for the lost, recover the stragglers, bandage the hurt, strengthen the sick, lead the strong and healthy to play, and give us nourishment. When we accept Jesus Christ as our Lord and Savior, He will dwell with us as our personal Shepherd!

QUESTIONS TO CONSIDER

- How can you use this promise (Ezekiel 34:11-16) to encourage a fellow Christian who is going through trials and tough times?

  _____

  _____

  _____

  _____

- Think of a personal experience of being sought and found by the Lord, and then share it with someone.

FOLLOW-UP

Who will care for us? Jesus Christ will! There are five New Testament passages that describe Christ as the Shepherd:

- Luke 15:3-7---A Shepherd seeking to find his lost sheep.

- John 10:1-18---A good Shepherd who lays his life down for us.

- Hebrews 13:20---The Great Shepherd.

- 1 Peter 2:25---The Shepherd of our souls.

- Revelation 7:17---The Lamb who will be our Shepherd.

GOD LOVES YOU, REGARDLESS

"The Lord is compassionate and merciful, slow to get angry and filled with unfailing love" Psalm 103:8.

OBJECTIVES OF THIS CHAPTER

- To learn ways to show appreciation and thanksgiving to God for His love and mercy.

- To accept the power of God's love and forgiveness.

- To think about loved ones and friends that are lost and the consequences of not knowing Christ as a Personal Savior.

- To examine your own life and ask if it's a true reflection of God's love.

CENTRAL TRUTH

No one can find peace for themselves unless they accept the fact they're lost and that God has provided peace through Christ.

Where would we be if God, the Higher Power, gave us what we deserved? To be faithful to the truth about God, we must hold equally to both God's judgment on all of us and to His continual reaching out to save all of us. God would be less than what He claims in the Bible if He were to judge and not redeem. The same is true if He were to redeem and not judge. Both of these aspects describe His nature and His character that affect all of us.

The Bible is very plain about the consequences of sin. But if a person is continually beat over the head with a Bible telling them how God will punish them for their sin and never told of God's love in spite of the sin, they're unlikely to be converted to faith in Christ. On the other hand, if all a person is told about God is His "come as you are" love, they're not likely to turn to Christ for forgiveness and pardon from the guilt produced by their sin.

As with so many of the Psalms written by David, he thanks God for all his blessings in Psalm 103.

Then he turns the thought to the gracious truth that God has not treated him the way he deserves to be treated.

"The Lord is compassionate and merciful, slow to get angry and filled with unfailing love" Psalm 103:8

There are four facts about God stated in Psalm 103:8: His mercy, His grace, His slowness to anger, and His steadfast love. When you consider these four attributes of God they show the overwhelming impact they have on God's desire to do something about the sad predicament of His people.

Do you think this is what society actually understands God to be? Or do they have a warped view of God? The culture of the day portrays God as a "mean old man" or as a "gentle Santa Clause". The Higher Power can't be adequately or correctly described in relation to a world's viewpoint. As Christians wanting to be on mission for Christ, we should spend time finding out what people really think about God. There are not many communication outlets that are committed to explaining the truth of what God is like.

QUESTIONS TO CONSIDER

- What's your brief definition of the four facts of God and how they affect you:

⇒ His mercy:

_____

_____

_____

⇒ His grace:

_____

_____

_____

⇒ His slowness to anger:

_____

_____

_____

⇒ His steadfast love:

_____

_____

_____

The facts of Scripture and the acts of history prove that God does not act the way people do. God's love is shown in His attitude toward this sinful generation. His holiness is not vindictive and it's not full of revenge and hatred. The Scriptures explain that God does not stay angry with us because of our sin and mistakes. He convicts us through His

Spirit and rightfully accuses us for our wrongs. And He gives us the chance to repent and ask for forgiveness. If we were to continue in disobedience and sin despite knowing it was wrong, then we bring judgment on ourselves. The Scripture gives many examples of God's judgment against sin. And Jesus Christ had words to say about the terrors of eternal judgment. We have been warned! Thank God for the warning and thank God that Jesus paid the price for our sin so that we can know His love and have fellowship with God.

A full experience of God's love includes that once we are forgiven of our sins God does not mete out punishment equal to our sins. Because of our sin we deserve to be punished, but God has taken upon Himself to offer a way out.

QUESTIONS TO CONSIDER

• **Is it enough to tell people about these four facts of God?**

_____

_____

_____

_____

• **What is it in your life that would lead a person to believe that what you're saying about God is really true?**

_____

_____

_____

_____

- **What does the constant acknowledgment of God's love and mercy do for you?**

_____

_____

_____

_____

I've known preachers in my lifetime to preach sin, hell, and eternal damnation every time they're in the pulpit. While I believe these three things are real, I also believe in God's love and care. There must be a healthy balance of all that the Bible teaches. I also believe it would help our Christian families if more of God's love was emphasized to make children unafraid to come to God when they're making mistakes and learning how to cope with positive life choices.

Scripture tells us that God's love is as high as the Heavens:

"For his unfailing love toward those who fear Him is as great as the height of the heavens above the earth"

Psalm 103:11.

This kind of love out distances anything that our minds can begin to conceive. God's love is beyond scope, in what it encompasses by endurance and strength. It's unending and it even extends to the most miserable people that you can think of. Love must be strong if it is to reach people in their deepest needs.

A true realization and acceptance of God's love comes with a fear of God. This is not a "fear or terror", but one of respect and honor because of who God is. A person must acknowledge God as the one and only Higher Power. For if one doesn't, it isn't God's love they will experience, only His judgment.

I've always enjoyed church and the worship experience with other people, but I feel closest to God when I'm in nature. From the beaches to the mountains, the city to the country, God can be seen everywhere! God declares to us "As far as the east is from the west" He will remove our sins if we humble ourselves and confess them. The point here is that God will not cause our sins to come back and haunt us. God's forgiving love will give a tremendous sense of release and freedom from guilt. Consequences from our sins may have to be dealt with. But even with them, when we confess our sin, God is willing to forgive, and we become clean to enjoy fellowship with the Lord. The Bible says:

"As a father pities his children, so the Lord pities those who fear Him" Psalm 103:13

To pity someone is not to appear weak. It means

compassion! It's also more than feeling sorry. It's going out and doing something for the one who's suffering. Do you suffer in the face of life's realities? We all do! God's compassion caused Him to send His Son, Jesus Christ, to enter into humankinds suffering.

What a human father does for his children is a small representation of this. My daughter once asked me what she would have to do for me to disown her. She asked in a joking way, but she was also indirectly testing the limitations of my love for her. I told her I would always love her, but she would have to deal with the consequences if she broke the rules! I've always had a strong attachment to my kids and I've used prayer and tough love to deal with their mistakes. I think of this and I'm reminded that God's love is even greater. The proof of that fact is found in the Book of Romans:

"God showed His great love for us by sending Christ to die for us while we were still sinners"
Romans 5:8.

Scripture explains in Genesis that humankind is made from the dust of the ground (Genesis 2:7). So, Psalm 103:14 explains very simply that God knows us because He made us. God doesn't expect more from us that we are able to produce. God doesn't expect us to do the impossibilities on our own. Coupled with His love and power we can achieve much more than we can on our own. Knowing our limitations and sinful mistakes God still loves us.

QUESTIONS TO CONSIDER

- What is an everyday illustration of God's love?

  _____

  _____

  _____

  _____

- What was it about God's love that convinced you to accept Christ as Savior?

  _____

  _____

  _____

  _____

- In what ways do some Christians find it hard to accept God's love, especially after they've sinned?

  _____

  _____

  _____

  _____

- What does Satan try to convince Christians of after they've sinned?

  _____

  _____

  _____

- **What would you suggest to help a Christian who carries a burden of guilt for past sins?**

_____

_____

_____

_____

Throughout history and in the lives of all who live, God's blessings have been tied to humankind's obedience. Punishment is enacted against disobedience. When Jesus came to earth, lived, and died for us, there was no question that God loved us. Now, because of Christ's resurrection, we have a blessed hope in which we can face the future. Christ came because God loved. In fact, the giving of His Son is the measure of God's love!

God loved people even before Jesus came to earth. It's just they were not aware of an all-encompassing love as was revealed by Jesus Christ. A new dimension of God's love was added for everyone everywhere to see. This dimension of His love touches us all. How can we understand and appreciate the depth of His love? When we read: "God gave His only Son", we get only a glimpse and can't thoroughly get the full meaning. There was an infinite cost so that the world could see the Father's love.

To feel this love we have to enter into the relationship of the Father-Son connection. We have to do this because the world is condemned and perishing. Without exercising saving personal faith in Christ, a person will continue to perish and be lost forever. They can't be saved by anything they do, no matter how moral, kind, or religious they claim to be. Many times true love is ignored, abused, and unappreciated. God's love can't be fully known and valued unless it's seen against the backdrop of perishing forever.

The alternative to perishing is eternal life. Jesus describes this in the Gospel of John:

"This is the way to eternal life; to know you, the only true God, and Jesus Christ, the one You sent to earth"
John 17:3.

Everlasting life begins for a person when they choose to believe in Jesus Christ. For the abundant life to be realized and experienced, believing in Christ has to be more than accepting the facts that he lived, died, and rose again. The eternal life begins for you when you totally trust yourself to Christ. It's an intentional act on your behalf whereby you ask for his forgiveness and invite him to be your Lord and Savior. This is the only way to know God personally.

God's love stands before us free and willing to give hope to a soul that knows there is no hope in this world beyond that humankind can do for us.

Doctors can extend a physical existence. But even in that thought, people are limited in their conscious living. We are all condemned by our sin and unbelief. The purpose of Christ's coming is to show the way out of that condemnation.

QUESTIONS TO CONSIDER

- **How can a Christian's actions show God's self-giving love for the sake of those that are not saved?**

_____

_____

_____

_____

- **What will it take on the part of Christians to convince the world that God really cares?**

_____

_____

_____

_____

FOLLOW-UP

The crucial problem today for the young and old is the fact they feel like there is no one to love them as they are. They find themselves lonely with no hope or purpose. The message of God's everlasting saving love must be carried to these people, many of whom have no church family or rarely attend church. Christians must carry this love to them. Otherwise, truth of God's love is only a theory. They must see that love in action!

GOD WORKS THROUGH ME

"Not by might, nor by power, but by my Spirit, says the Lord of hosts." Zechariah 4:6

OBJECTIVES OF THIS CHAPTER

- To understand the spiritual principle of how God works.

- To accept that human ability alone counts for nothing in doing God's work.

- To ask the Holy Spirit to give the needed power to overcome sin and to do Christian service.

- To consider what work is yet to be done by dedicated and yielded Christians.

CENTRAL THEME

People can be useful channels for the accomplishment of God's work, if they surrender completely to God for the infilling of His Spirit.

One of the hardest concepts to accept is that something can come from nothing. There were no pre-existing materials for God to use when He made the universe. He started with nothing but His omnipotence. From that time until now, God has been demonstrating this same principle for the world to see. In the Old Testament He took a band of slaves out of Egypt and made a nation out of people who had nothing and considered themselves nothing until God gave them hope. God is still the same. For the New Testament principle states it this way:

"God chose what is weak in the world to shame the strong. He chose things that are powerless to shame those who are powerful. God chose things despised by the world; things counted as nothing at all, and used them to bring to nothing what the world considers important. As a result, no one can ever boast in the presence of God" 1 Corinthian 1:27-29.

What seems to be the battle is the "pride of people" versus the "honor and glory of God". People's pride leads them to believe that they can do anything by their own power. God, acting as the Higher Power, consistently refutes our pride by doing things in the opposite ways from the world view. God works power through weakness. He baffles peoples mind because He continues to accomplish something out of nothing. Compared to the majesty of God, the Bible says:

"All the nations of the world are but a drop in the bucket. They are nothing more than dust on the scales" Isaiah 40:15.

Yet God considers us His crowning creation. He says:

"You are fearfully and wonderfully made" Psalm 139:14.

The supreme example of humankind's weakness and God's power is the Cross. Man's power put Jesus to death. Jesus had to suffer as a weak man; subject to the great political power of the day. But out of that weakness, God worked the greatest power of all: power over sin and death! Behind all human power aligned against God is the power of Satan. Check the score and we know that Satan was defeated at the Cross. When Jesus came out of the grave alive, he proved what great things God can do out of seeming weakness. This same principle must work in us. All of us must crucify our own power so that God's power can be demonstrated in our nothingness!

There once was a priest and prophet named Zechariah that lived hundreds of years ago. He grew up during the rebuilding of Jerusalem before Christ came on the scene. Zechariah was very perceptive and had a sense of personal involvement with the needs of his people. God called him to be a spokesman in the context of the people's struggle to establish their spiritual foundation and relationship to God and His law.

All of the prophets during the Old Testament period had to insist that there were legitimate moral reasons because of their plight. It wasn't an accident in history that they faced their own destruction. God's holiness was consistently at work in their lives. God's "anger" toward sin was a result of the people's will and God's nature to discipline those He loved.

God's wrath is not comparable to a human's ill feelings or bad tempers. People usually get angry when they're offended or hurt. Many times human anger results in further sin. This doesn't happen with God. From the very beginning, God has consistently warned everyone that disobedience would bring judgment. This judgment can be personal and national suffering.

Every generation needs to be taught this truth about God: He's holy and requires obedience from His people. The tragedy in this is people many times chose punishment rather than blessing. God warns us of the dangers of disobedience. But He always counteracts His message by telling us, in the Bible, there are blessings to be given in obedience. In other words, when a person says no to God, they're also saying no to their own best interest. The devil's lie is that we're better off if we go our own way and disregard the ways of the Lord. The truth is that if we follow God we're better off all-around.

After explaining God's anger because of their life of sin Zechariah called the people to repent of their past sins. The Bible says God's message came to him:

"Therefore say to the people: Return to Me and I will return to you" Zechariah 1:4.

"Return to me" is a description and a call to repentance. "I will return to you" is a promise of the Lord's presence and blessing. In Zechariah's day, this was a necessary step spiritually so that God's people would be in the right frame of mind and God's wonderful plan for them could be revealed.

God does show anger, but it's just a sketch as compared to the background of His love. Wrath and grace co-exist in God. If we fail to explain the anger He has for sin, then we overlook the truth. People can be lead astray to their own peril if they don't understand God will absolutely not tolerate sin. We cripple our use in God's Kingdom if we don't have the proper perspective about the consequences of sin in our life. Yet, if we fail to explain God's love for sinners, we leave people with a misrepresented view of God and no hope for salvation. God's anger is what makes salvation necessary and it's His love that makes salvation possible.

The hope on which we as Christians stand is that Christ took the judgment we deserved. Jesus Christ satisfied God's holiness, so that we can be forgiven and restored to fellowship with the Lord. In this modern world, God has come to us in Christ and made it possible to live a life of meaning and purpose. God, who is the Higher Power, has pictured Himself as the father of the prodigal son, waiting for us to return to Him so that we can be made useful to Him. Repentance is that return!

QUESTIONS TO CONSIDER

- **Why do people sometimes fail to make the connection between God's anger toward sin and the consequences they may be suffering?**

_____

_____

_____

_____

- **What are some sins in your own life that you need to repent of? Meditate silently about**

these things.

_____

_____

_____

_____

- **If we know that God extends His forgiving love to us in Christ, what makes it hard for us to repent?**

_____

_____

_____

_____

Throughout the later chapters in Zechariah, he has several dreams or visions which we're confusing enough that Zechariah needed help in figuring out what they meant. The visions were unique in that they showed the direct provision that can come to God's people, like you and me. The indwelling power of the Holy Spirit is what provides to us what we need to accomplish His will. Those provisions could be wisdom, something material, or just the cooperative work of a few people who are unified in purpose.

The Holy Spirit's work is to take of the riches of Christ and minister them to each Christian's needs. Is there a need in your life? Have your sins been properly dealt with through confession and repentance. God works through all of us even in the small ways. God will take our willingness to do the small things and make them even more influential than others may imagine possible. We must consider all weak things as to be the potential glue that can hold the bigger parts together. God tells us He doesn't despise anything, no matter its size, as long as it's being done for His glory. God will accept our works if they're done in clear allegiance to Christ. It's by our works we are known and it's our little works that can call out others to get involved.

It's important to remember that no job for the cause of Christ can be accomplished by strength and power alone. No physical or mental power alone can do the jobs to which we are called. God's work has to be done by more than human force or abilities.

"Not by might, nor by power, but by My Spirit, says the Lord" Zechariah 4:6.

This is the underlying reason why our sin must be dealt with (confession, repentance, and forgiveness) before we can have the fullness of God's Spirit to achieve all He intends for us to do. God works through us. And our anointing is supplied by the Spirit of God!

It doesn't matter how much we have or how little. What matters is how much we give of ourselves! This is real ministry! When we agree to commit and choose to give ourselves completely, it's God's responsibility to refill us with His Spirit. And He will! It's called the Spirit-filled life! The main spiritual issue is that God can work to save His people and He offers us salvation through His Son, Jesus Christ. "He gives power to the faint and to them that have no might He increases strength" How? By His Spirit!

People must decide if they'll trust the Lord to get the work done, and look to Him alone, or whether they'll try to do His work with human resources alone. Jesus said:

"Apart from me you can do nothing" John 15:5

"Shouts of grace" should come forth from God's children as He strategically places us where He wants us. How much we all owe glory to God because of His grace!

FOLLOW-UP

The church and individual Christians face the temptation to rely on human strength for their own needs and for the program s of the church. God chooses to work not through our human abilities, but according to human self-sacrifice and self-discipline. A person's human weakness is no obstacle to the Lord, but their unwillingness to be a yielded vessel is! "God's power is made perfect in weakness." But our lives, weak or strong, must be given over to the Lord for His use.

GOD SPEAKS TO ME THROUGH CHRIST

"No one has ever seen God. But Christ has made God known to us" John 1:18

OBJECTIVES OF THIS CHAPTER

- To grasp the full significance of God's speaking through Christ.

- To use everything Christ has to offer for our needs.

- To share with others what God has said and done through Christ.

- To always consider what Christ would do in church life and personal life situations.

CENTRAL TRUTH

God's message in Christ is absolutely clear, but people will not understand unless they respond with wholehearted obedience.

What would we know about God if Christ had never come? Through Scripture, God's power and deity could be "clearly perceived" in the things that have been made. We are truly a people without excuse!

"For ever since the world was created, people have seen the earth and sky. Through everything God made, they can clearly see His invisible qualities — His eternal power and divine nature. So they have no excuse for not knowing God" Romans 1:20"

The apostle Paul said this would be sufficient for a person to honor God and desire to give thanks. Your common sense might lead you to think a Higher Power or something of greater intelligence than humans made the world.

Once while on a military mission, an Army Colonel told our unit, "In all of time, in all of history, at some point everyone that has life longs for a relationship with a Higher Power." I wrote that quote down because of the impact it made upon me. I agree with him. The problem is that many people will not humble themselves to seek the Higher Power. They go through life trying to make it or they attach themselves to a weak, temporary, fantasy source of so-called spiritual power.

So, what more do we know about God since Jesus Christ has come? We see the greatness and divinity of God in the powerful works Jesus did. But in addition he gave us the hopefulness that God cares about all of us as specific individuals. Jesus' message is that we are worth something to God and He goes to extreme lengths to bring these people into a personal relationship with Himself.

Jesus repeatedly did rounds of "show and tell" giving evidence of God's love and holiness. He also proved the rewards that come with faith and the punishment that comes with rebellion. A majority of Christ's work consisted of instructing people how to pray to God as their Heavenly Father, how to confess their sins to Him, and what they can do to have a continual supply of God's power in their lives.

If Jesus hadn't come the first time we would have no knowledge of how to pray, how to confess, and how to draw upon the Higher Power. These are not the only benefits of knowing about Christ, but just the beginning about the abundant life that Jesus shared.

The climax of Jesus' mission was his death and resurrection. But his ultimate revelation was this statement:

"Whoever has seen me, has seen the Father (God)"
John 14:8.

Christians with full assurance and complete confidence can share the wonderful news that God is not some far-off, out-of-touch deity. He is revealed by His creation and can be known through an encounter with His Son, Jesus Christ!

Every Christian and person who wonders will be short-changed if they don't grasp the truth of the following passage:

"Long ago God spoke to our early fathers in many different ways. He spoke through the early preachers. But in these last days He has spoken to us through His Son. God gave His Son everything. It was by His Son that God made the world. The Son shines with the shining-greatness of the Father. The Son is as God is in every way. It is the Son Who holds up the whole world by the power of His Word. The Son gave His own life so we could be clean from all sin. After He had done that, He sat down on the right side of God in heaven"
Hebrews 1:1-3.

This passage is crucial to a person's knowledge and appreciation of Jesus Christ as Savior. It shows Jesus' exalted position, his nature, and what God appointed him to do.

It was through prophets like Moses, Isaiah, Haggai, Jeremiah, Ezekiel, Obadiah, Zephaniah, Zechariah, Malachi, and others that were God's instruments of self-revelation. What God wanted the people to know He revealed to them through chosen men. God spoke through mercy and judgment of sin, but it was the duty of the prophets to tell what these instances meant and the purposes behind them.

God spoke in storms, thunder, audible voices, dreams, and visions. None of the prophets were ever given the entirety of God's message at one time. God gave them inward suggestions at times which sometimes required them to ask for confirmation. When Jesus came to earth he inaugurated a new era of time that would warn that the world as we know it will not last forever. The universe was assigned to Christ as His Kingdom. This Kingdom, of which God made, includes everything in time and space, people as well as things, material, spiritual existence in the physical world past, present, and future.

Scriptures reveal that the Son has a majestic position:

"The Word (Christ) was in the beginning. The Word was with God. The Word was God. He was with God in the beginning. He made all things. Nothing was made without Him making it" John 1:1-3.

Jesus not only created the world with God, he sustains it by the words he spoke. His word was so far-reaching, that it applies to everyone that has ever been born to the present day. Jesus' words are sustaining. The whole world is truly in his hands as far as the future is concerned.

QUESTIONS TO CONSIDER

- Is there some sin you desire to be released from?

  _____

  _____

  _____

  _____

- Is there some concern about the future that's too big for you to carry?

  _____

  _____

  _____

  _____

- Do you know somebody who doubts Christ's ability to save? If so, is it because they don't know enough about him?

  _____

  _____

  _____

  _____

- Do you think people are in need because they don't ask him to help or believe he can help?

  _____

  _____

  _____

- **What do we seem to talk about more than we talk about Christ? Social problems? Politics? Our problems? Why is this?**

Anyone who reads the Gospels of Matthew and Luke will know the record of the one who was born physically the same as everyone else, but from an ancestry that's timeless and divine. The Gospel of Mark begins with his baptism and temptation. John goes back to eternity past and links Jesus with God. Jesus was far more than just a man of Nazareth. Jesus was the eternal Word of God!

John the apostle wrote the most profound theological description of Christ. He called him "The Word". Jesus was marked and identified in this way:

"The Word became flesh and dwelt among us, full of grace and truth" John 1:14.

"Word" is logos in Greek and it can mean a thought or concept, and the expression or utterance of that thought. Christ in the flesh is the physical expression of what God is. He could be called the collective thought of God, in which all of God's wisdom is embodied. The divine word had to be expressed for all to be able to see, so it became flesh in the person of

Jesus Christ.

It's important that a person understands "The Word" was fully God and not some lesser person of distinction. The unique Trinity relationship---Father (God), Son (the Word), and Holy Spirit will always baffle even the most intelligent. The facts of the Bible stand by themselves. And there's no reason to try and prove them. It's a fact that each part of the Trinity is an inherent deity in his own right. There's nothing of lesser value or importance about the Word or of the Spirit.

Christ is called the Son of God and had full powers of the Father. However, in his human (fleshly) state he voluntarily relinquished some of his divine authority, but he never became less than God. It's obvious that Jesus' expression of God in the flesh began when he was born. We celebrate this time at Christmas. But Christ had no temporal beginning. He always existed with the Father.

"The Word (Christ) was in the beginning. The Word was with God. The Word was God" John 1:1.

It's really impossible to describe this with any human concepts that are understandable by anyone. We have the Bible to read and to trust as truth. It's one of the acts of faith we must live---trusting God at His Word. Jesus once gave us a glimpse of his relation to God in a prayer:

*"Now, Father, honor me with the honor I had with You
before the world was made" John 17:5.*

This is a deep mystery! But one that draws us
back to learn more and more and causes us to re-
quest that He show us more truth as we love Him
more each day. The basic fact of Scripture is that the
Trinity: Father, Son, and Holy Spirit is a relation that
defies any human logic. This is where we live by
faith and can take heart and hope in the divine help
that comes to us through three channels of deity.

There's no reason to argue the validity of this
power structure nor should we dismiss the Trinity
as irrelevant simply because we can't describe it. Rather, the appropriate response is to admit the limits
of our human minds and praise Him in thanks for
revealing Himself in three persons. Reinforcing everything Jesus said and did in the special relation he
had with God the Father; Christ's life must always
be understood and interpreted in that light.

When John writes:

*"He made all things. Nothing was made without Him
making it. Life began by Him. His Life was the Light for
men. The Light shines in the darkness. The darkness has
never been able to put out the Light" John 1:3-5.*

We can associate creation with God the Son. This
thought gives light to the truth that Jesus brought
life into being. He gave it to human kind. His life

brought light to all of us. This applies physically and spiritually and says that all of us owe our physical existence to Christ. In his death and resurrection, Jesus offers everyone a different kind of life. Christians owe their spiritual life to Christ. All humans have physical life, but not all have spiritual life. The world is dead in trespasses and sin as a whole and only those who trust in Christ receive everlasting spiritual life. Jesus went about talking about never-ending, abundant life and said he was The Way for a person to obtain this kind of life.

Left to public opinion, people thought Jesus was a carpenter, a crazy man, a fool, a troublemaker. But as the Higher Power, God sent someone to be a witness to the truth of who he was. This witness was none other than John the Baptist. John the apostle, writer of the gospel, pronounced that John the Baptist was sent by God on his mission, and that his mission was to testify to the light, Jesus Christ. It was an effective witness and stirred the people to make a decision whether to follow or not.

What impresses the most is not the words Christ spoke, but his acts and deeds. He showed graciousness and truthfulness to perfection. He brings saving grace to all who will believe and he reveals the truth about God. The net result is a beautiful example of how we are to love one another and treat each other with respect and dignity. Christ doesn't come to us as a harsh task-master, but one who offers you and me everlasting life!

Above Christ's words and because of his actions, he has enabled us to know and seek to understand the Higher Power, which is God the Father. We see God when we look at Christ and we're given access to our Heavenly Father by virtue of Christ's death and resurrection.

QUESTIONS TO CONSIDER

- **The evidence for God is so overwhelming in the person of Christ, why do you think people refuse that evidence?**

_____

_____

_____

_____

- **What have you been doing to give testimony of Christ?**

_____

_____

_____

- **God has spoken. How are people going to hear what He has said if Christians don't tell them?**

_____

_____

_____

_____

5 POINTS TO REMEMBER

- In Christ's birth, you can see the power of God to rise above the natural and manifest himself in a miraculous way!

- In Christ's life, you can see the nature and characteristics of God at work!

- In Christ's death, you can see the sacrifice of God to redeem lost people!

- In Christ's resurrection, ascension, and intercession you can see God as mighty, ruling, and victorious!

- In Christ's coming again, you can see the cleansing and ruling Christ!

FOLLOW-UP

We can only stand amazed at the wonder of all Christ said and did. The words he spoke and the stories he told don't do him justice. So many false and partial impressions are given of him that it's rare to get the full scope of his personality and service. Spending time in prayer and reading the Bible will help you get to know the real Jesus and will subsequently help you understand the Higher Power. The timeline of his life begins with pre-existent Creator to eternal magnificent Savior and mediator. We limit our own life if we slight any aspect of him. One day, as he promised, he will come back to earth and then the full knowledge and power of him will be revealed to all.

GOD'S POWER WILL SUSTAIN ME TO THE END

"My grace is all you need. My power works best in weakness. So now I am glad to boast about my weaknesses, so that the power of Christ can work through me" II Corinthians 12:9.

OBJECTIVES OF THIS CHAPTER

- To learn about God's promise of strength.

- To develop stronger "faith muscles" to believe the promise.

- To see weaknesses and failures not as the end of the story, but as an open door to God's opportunity.

- To determine how to use Christ's power in a person's daily life.

CENTRAL TRUTH

There's a greater tragedy than being a defeated Christian. It's being defeated because God's way to victory was not used.

Perhaps the hardest concept for a non-Christian to accept is how strength can come from weakness. This is because from a secular viewpoint there's no substitute for visible strength and power. The world and all its vanity thinks you must act from a position of strength to accomplish anything. The thought is you can't do anything if you're weak and powerless.

One reason that Jesus Christ is considered a stumbling block is because the Cross is a symbol of weakness. Jesus never moved from a position of human strength and it's considered that human strength put him to death on the cross.

Because Jesus had no economic or political base and no friends of influence he was considered a threat or nuisance, at best, to the Roman government and religious leaders. Even the massive crowds that followed him couldn't exercise power. The authoritarian power was in the hands of the Jewish religion ruling insiders and in the hands of the Roman emperor.

Yet out of that seeming weakness and defeat God unleashed the greatest power the world has ever seen: power over sin and death. The power of sin is stronger than any person. And there's never been anyone to defeat death other than Christ. When Jesus willingly suffered at the hands of human power, he made it possible for all his followers to gain access to divine power after the resurrection.

The secret, since revealed, is that divine power is available to the weak, those who admit to themselves that they are defeated by sin and death. The pattern that Jesus established is so God's power could come into human lives and change them. Victory follows admission of defeat. And power, through Christ comes to those who have no power in themselves. One day the world's way will be turned upside down.

"God blesses those who are humble, for they will inherit the whole earth" Matthew 5:5.

Scripture has long been the encouraging word for God's children. And the following found in Isaiah is some of the best:

"To whom will you compare me? Who is my equal asks the Holy One. Look up into the Heavens. Who created all the stars? He brings them out like an army, one after another, calling each by its name. Because of His great power and incomparable strength, not a single one is missing" Isaiah 40:25-26.

God's great power is available to anyone as long as they are His children. Think for a moment. What alternatives are there apart from God? There are many to choose from! There are practical atheists who act as though there is no God, so why bother trying to find a comparison? There are scores of people who live by chance and fate. They talk about luck and destiny, not about a personal God. Is there a "safe bet" when it comes to personal beliefs? The answer is yes when it begins with "In Christ"!

The prevailing thought today is that God is being compared with two other universal belief systems: atheism and agnosticism. Either there is no God, or if there is a God we can't be sure about it. Those are the choices a person must make. The Christian confidently contends that neither atheism nor agnosticism can be compared intellectually or in terms of personal spiritual satisfaction with the Holy, powerful, loving God of the Bible. But they are compared by all who are uncomfortable with giving up their right to themselves.

In Isaiah God asks for a person to look up at the stars and ask who made them. God answers his own question by saying He made them and named them all (v. 26). Of course there are some people who look up into space and don't find God there at all. The prevailing idea in scientific thought is by chance the stars just happened to come together with various combinations of the right elements. What God intended to be proof of His power and majesty has been either denied by human authority or twisted by magic and superstition.

QUESTIONS TO CONSIDER

- **What obstacles have you encountered when you tried to share your belief in God?**

  blame game, avoid topic, business of life

- **Is there an answer good enough for the person who prefers to believe in chance?**

  not really, you can't convience someone who ~~doesen't~~ dosen't want to know the truth.

- **If we can't convince a person to accept the evidence for God in the world around them, what other evidence or testimony can we give?**

  - your personal testimony
  - have them read the Word and respond what they glean from it

The familiar account put forth by non-believers and some discouraged Christians is that God doesn't know about us and He doesn't care. Some people think that God is hidden and disregards the troubles we have to face. God asks us another question:

"Why do you talk that way? How can you say I don't see your troubles?" Isaiah 40:27 ⌒

Personally, I feel it's helpful for the discouraged and downtrodden to write down exactly why they feel despair and left alone. Identifying the problem is the first step in finding a solution. What are the outward circumstances that led you to feel this way? What was it that led you to think that God doesn't care? Out of this experience of self-examination you can receive light and strength from above.

God is the everlasting God. He is timeless. There never was a time without God. He's always been self-existent. God made everything. It may seem strange to speak of God this way---in human terms. But our perceptions are hard-wired this way.

"The Lord is the everlasting God, the creator of all the earth. He never grows weak or weary. No one can measure the depths of His understanding. He gives power to the weak and strength to the powerless" Isaiah 40:28-31. ⌒

We simply can't understand all there is about a Higher Power and what He does. If it seems He withdraws His hand of care, to allow us to walk alone in darkness, there's a reason for it known only to Him. We would save ourselves much trouble and worry if we questioned less and accepted more. This isn't easy. But that's the stuff faith is made of.

One of the greatest joys I have as a pastor is to hear the praise reports of my church members. Remarkable are the testimonies of those who have said that when they felt at the lowest point, unable to endure one more day, God came through and fulfilled the promises. Picture yourself flying above the troubles that plague you by reading and meditating on this Scripture:

"But they who wait upon the Lord will get new strength. They will soar high on wings like eagles. They will run and not grow weary. They will walk and not faint"
Isaiah 40:31.

A person may need spiritual strength because they are suffering physical weakness. God will give strength of spirit, even though He may not heal their body. Most doctors know that a strong spirit is helpful to physical healing. What an encouragement it is to our spirits when we feel better physically. Our needs are total and so are God's provisions.

God's gift of strength is not so that we can be removed from all problems that get in our way. The world doesn't change from day to day and neither will our problems just disappear. What does change is our weakness and weariness. They are changed into strength and power so that we can "run" and "walk" through the battles of life without being overcome by fatigue.

The one condition given in Isaiah 40 specified for our receiving the strength of the Lord: It's waiting for Him (v. 31). Rather than complain, we must wait. Waiting is hard! Waiting can be active and sometimes it can take on a passive effect. One side of waiting is found in Exodus 14:13:

"Just stand still and watch the Lord rescue you today."

The other way is found in Exodus 14:15:

⟶*"Tell the people of Israel to go forward."* ⟵

Both ways require doses of faith and patience.

The Key to waiting seems to be using the time to think about God and His character. Go over in your mind how He helped others and desires to help you. Recall the times He has helped you. Thank Him for every blessing you can think of. Human problems diminish or grow smaller when you focus your thoughts on what all God has done for you and promises to do. That's part of receiving strength from the Lord as the Higher Power!

QUESTIONS TO CONSIDER

- Share a recent experience of receiving God's strength.

  difficulties at work

- Why is it good to be reminded of the basic facts about God?

  to give Hope in a hopeless state

- What is it in your experience that keeps you from applying these facts to your problems?

  self-service
  relying on self too much

- How can overwork and too many activities, even church activities, be a means of draining spiritual vitality?

  can bring about bitterness

The apostle Paul had many needs and depended on God and the people who loved him to pass along their sincere help. When Paul was unjustly jailed and in a tight situation, he had all the ingredients for a classic blow up: negligence, misunderstandings, and sufferings. What was Paul's secret of deliverance from defeat and despair? He didn't complain of want. He came to realize that complaining never helped. Complaining usually reflects unbelief in God's wisdom and love. Paul stated:

∿ *"I've learned, in whatever state I am, to be content"* ❦
Philippians 4:11.

Can we really be happy with what we have, or don't have? We bring trouble on ourselves because we itch for something. Being content regardless of our circumstances, really means being content with and thankful for whatever it is God has brought our way. When Jesus becomes personal to us, his power is made real and is applied to our most pressing needs. Christ's indwelling power is possible at all phases of our life---in good times as well as bad!

⌐ *"I can do all things because Christ gives me the strength"*
Philippians 4:13. ⌐

As we contemplate the use of God's sustaining, renewing power, we must apply it not only to our weaknesses. These times are frequently tests of our reliance upon God. Beware of slipping into thinking that if we have everything, we don't need Christ. Never look at your obstacles as a hindrance to all that you've wished and prayed for, but see them as opportunities to unleash Christ's power in your life. If you do this you will be a witness to God's sustaining grace. Learn by your experiences to draw upon the Higher Power. This happens by simply talking to the Lord, telling how you feel, and asking him for a fresh supply of strength for the day. Christ's strength at sometimes comes through other people. This means you can also be used by Him to help others find strength and hope.

QUESTIONS TO CONSIDER

- **Is it possible to be content in all circumstances? Why or why not?**

  Yes, when you know and affirm that God loves you.

- **In the past week, on what occasion did you draw on Christ's strength?**

  uncertainty of Haley and Daniel situation

- Think about your problems now. How can you
  use Christ's power in these circumstances?

trust His plan
trust His timing
remember what you have
to be thankful for, remember
how it could be worse

FOLLOW-UP

Many people are moved emotionally when they think of breaking out of their ordinary existence to attempt brilliant, brave exploits. God doesn't offer His children an "impossible dream". He offers a "possible dream" that can become a reality if we would just follow a simple plan: *"Ask and what you are asking for will be given to you. Look and what you are looking for you will find. Knock and the door you are knocking on will be opened to you"* Matthew 7:7.

THE PRIORITY OF GOD IN MY LIFE

"You must not have any other god but Me" Exodus 20:3

OBJECTIVES OF THIS CHAPTER

- To beware of sharing divided loyalties with God.

- To overcome worry.

- To worship God from the highest spiritual motives because of Who He is and what He's done.

- To take a fresh look at the reasons Jesus gave for putting God first.

CENTRAL TRUTH

God demands undivided worship and the chief affection of our lives because it honors Him and brings blessings to us.

Everyone has an authority they must submit to. After working in a state correctional facility for twelve years I've seen first-hand how authority over another person works. And in some cases doesn't work! We recognize that every human condition must be governed by some authority. Someone has to be in the position to make final decisions. This is why schools have principals, armies have generals, corporations have presidents, prisons have wardens, and nations have presidents, prime ministers, kings, and dictators. All civilized countries understand and accept this as the price we pay to have order.

Because this is a common acceptance of most people, it's strange that many people don't accept this view of the world as a whole. Who's in charge? Who is the ultimate decision-maker? There have been some who appeared on the world's stage claiming they're the ones who run things. These people have set out to conquer and rule the world. Though they've tried, none has completely succeeded. In the process of this power grab, terrible disasters have been inflicted upon the world.

The Christian believes there's a Higher Power

who rules nature and the world. He is a supreme being; final authority. Even the most powerful human rulers hold their positions simply because God allows them to. The fact that these rulers don't honor God as God doesn't change their status of hierarchy.

There's a danger, in simply acknowledging that God is authoritative, while at the same time refusing to believe that He cares how we live. Because God is superior over all of us, He will make demands upon those that He created. People may think they live independently of any governing divine authority, and many people are doing that very thing, but God's will is not so easily flouted. Believers need to affirm the consequences, not only of unbelief, but also of refusing to listen to what God has to say. His commandments reveal His nature and what our response to that nature to Him must be.

God has a special relationship with His people. There were some very specific commands placed on His people years ago because of what He had done for them. In about 1441 B.C., while they were camped at Mount Sinai, God spoke some direct words. God said:

"You must not have any other god but Me" Exodus 20:3.

In this one verse, God makes it clear from the beginning that He is exclusive of all other gods. He doesn't just tolerate false religion and false gods, He forbids it! God doesn't share worship with other deities. The mixture of truth and error is prohibited. We should never try to bring God down to the level of idols and false gods. God is not one of equal authority on a buffet of choice gods! He is the Higher Power and the only true God!

Witnessing the Egyptians worship many gods, the Israelites, at times, had lapsed into idolatry and pagan worship. At that time, the fundamental issue in their minds was who is the true God? They had seen Him work, but saw the false gods be made alive by magicians, sorcery, and Satan's power. God's command for exclusive worship is based on His position as the Creator of humankind. Allegiance was owed to the Creator. God was the choice of Abraham and his descendants. God owned the Israelites in a special way; they were His people, therefore they had to worship Him.

The testimony of our day is to be the same as it was all those years ago. We are to be a witness to the fact of the existence of one true God. We are monotheists (worshippers of only one God). We are to be light-bearers to a world that's distracted by the worship of spirits, heavenly bodies, and other man-made idols. It's a complete waste of time to worship other gods. False worship leads to fear, uncertainty, and corruption of the worshippers. Nothing good comes from it. In fact, not only can it harm you, it stokes the wrath of God.

Listen to the words of God:

"You must not make for yourself an idol of any kind or an image of anything in the Heavens or on the earth or in the sea" Exodus 20:4.

People have an affinity for trinkets, what-knots, and small objects that represent some things they care for on a much larger scale. We must be careful not to make them objects of desire. False gods are the result of humankind's rejection of the truth, the creation of our insistent desire to worship something, even untruth!

God's command that forbids any likeness to be made of Him proves that God is beyond any human representation. When we worship God we are to do so in Spirit and in truth. God does not require physical aides to worship Him. The Christian emphasis is on the truthfulness and purity of worship from the heart and the mind.

It's always possible that some lesser god will sneak into our lives. It's a subtle happening and one that can easily happen without your own awareness. Anything that takes you away from God and removes God as the priority of your life is considered a god or an idol. The world, the culture, and liberal media make it easy to fall prey to divided loyalties.

This leads to foolish behavior, fear, superstition and degrading practices.

Christians will do themselves well by spending more time considering their choices. Being thankful to God continuously throughout our life helps deliver us from darkness and paganism. Thank God that He is pure, true, and Holy! What a blessing this is to us!

QUESTIONS TO CONSIDER

- **What are some human relationships that require exclusive commitments? Why are they worthwhile?**

_____

_____

_____

_____

- **Do you think that when Christians talk about God they give the impression that He requires exclusive, pure worship?**

_____

_____

_____

_____

- **What are some modern evidences of divided worship or loyalty?**

_____

_____

_____

_____

Early on in his ministry Christ laid down the spiritual principles of his Kingdom. Many of those principles were given in the "Sermon on the Mount" Jesus applied a valid principle of everyday life to spiritual affairs. He says:

"No one can serve two masters. For you will hate one and love the other; you will be devoted to one and despise the other" Matthew 6:24.

If you had to be accountable to two people at your job and one told you to do a task one way and the other one said something else, there's going to be a problem sooner or later. It's impossible to please everyone and when it comes to our life, we must choose to obey God or another master.

Naturally, we don't like Christ's all-or-nothing approach. We think we can pay our duties to God part of the time, and then do what we like the rest of the time. Not so, according to Jesus. We can make it easy or hard on ourselves. The decision to serve God eliminates trying to serve other masters.

The word "serve" means to belong wholly to, or to be entirely under the command of. It doesn't mean serving when you feel like it. The decision to serve God is one that we all must make on our own.

The sooner we do, the easier it is making the lesser choices in life.

Some of these decisions include husbands having to decide if their job or their family comes first. A businessman may have to decide whether or not to stick to his moral principles, even though it may cost him money. A teenager might have to decide whether it's worth losing some friends if he doesn't go along with the crowd. A Christian might have to choose between the risk of ridicule or stating a clear witness for Christ.

In the end, all choices boil down to the choice between God and something else. Each person must decide for themselves what's most important and what represents their highest favor. What are you really interested in? What do you live for? If anything (even worthwhile things) assumes a greater importance than serving God, then this has in effect ruled God out. We need to make the categories very clear, for many people are trying to straddle the fence between God and the world.

Nothing about the world can give you a permanent peace. But nothing of this world is secure; only temporal. So, the question arises out of our needy selves, if we don't place our relationships with God as the highest priority in life and serve Him, who shall provide all that we need? The reason many people make money and possessions their priority is because they have a weak faith in God to provide their needs. There comes a fear that originates from Satan that if we don't pursue things ourselves we'll go lacking and become less than ordinary.

Anxiety is one of the worst human conditions. It can destroy you mentally, emotionally, and physically. The primary cause of this is the fret and worry about material needs. We try to justify our anxiety about basic needs: what we will eat, drink, or wear. By extension, of course, we can apply it to anything: our jobs, our children, our health, and the list goes on. Jesus commands us not to be anxious.

"That is why I tell you not to worry about everyday life; whether you have enough food and drink, or enough clothes to wear. Isn't life more than food, and your body more than clothing. These things dominate the thoughts of unbelievers, but your Heavenly Father already knows all your needs" Matthew 6:25-32.

Jesus does more than tell us not to worry. He gives four reasons why:

1. Life really isn't our material existence. Most of our time and strength are consumed in providing these needs for ourselves and our children. Jesus doesn't deny that. Real life is found on another plane. Life does include the basic physical necessities, but there is a higher spiritual relation that

gives life its real meaning. Values as joy, serenity, beauty, peace, and forgiveness are not physical. A person may not have much in the way of material possessions but they may still enjoy life to the fullest. The meaning of life is found only in a relation of trust in God through Christ. Jesus came to give us abundant life. He told us that the only real life, eternal life, is to be found in knowing God. Therefore, if that is what life is really about, why should we worry on the purely physical level?

2. We're not to worry because we have ample evidence in nature that God will take care of us. Jesus talked about God's provision of food for birds and clothing for lilies. It's self-evident that there's a spiritual lesson here for all humankind. It's clear that God does have priorities. God has placed a higher value on people than He has on nature. We can depend on Him to give us the necessities of life.

3. According to Jesus, worry can't do you any good anyway. If worry could add something to your life, it would be worth it. But anxiety doesn't provide food and it can't make you better if you're sick. Instead, anxiety only makes us feel worse and sometimes can delay the healing we need.

4. Why worry if God knows your needs, He will

furnish them. The person who leaves out God has to work and worry because they think everything depends on them. It's a tremendous release when you realize that a living, Higher Power knows and cares about you. This frees you to be able to receive God's loving gifts without being tied in knots of anxiety.

The first thought of the person who isn't trusting in God is to figure out how they can provide for themselves. We have to reverse the order and put God first! Even above necessities, because it's an expression of our faith and obedience. If you really trust God, you'll make Him first in everything. We really should put God first because of Who He is. Jesus promised that if we put God first, we'll receive what brings our highest good. "All these things shall be yours!" God's gifts are not limited to material needs. He's richly blessed us beyond all of that.

What better way to be different than to put God's Kingdom and His righteousness ahead of everything else we might want for ourselves! Any Christian that chooses to do this, will stand-out above the crowd and be a bold, strong witness for others.

In the Bible, Joshua commanded:

"Choose today whom you will serve. As for me and my family, we will serve the LORD" Joshua 24:15.

If the church lacks a strong, clear-cut witness for God, it may be because her members don't yet have the single eye for God alone. Be victimized by worry no more! We need to pray for a new sense of confidence in the Lord, based on the facts given by Jesus Christ from the Holy Bible.

QUESTIONS TO CONSIDER

- **Write down all areas of your life in which you're trying to please more than one person.**

_____

_____

_____

_____

- **What action should you take to serve one or the other?**

_____

_____

_____

_____

- **What is holding you back from serving God alone?**

_____

_____

_____

- **Write down some of your fears and worries in the physical realm. Why do you worry about these things? Is it insufficient knowledge about**

God, or a lack of faith?

_____

_____

_____

_____

- **Are you really putting God first? If you aren't, think about how that would solve your anxieties.**

_____

_____

_____

FOLLOW-UP

The key to surviving your time on earth is making time for God. He must be first place in your life. We need a healthy dose of His grace daily! When we treat each new day as a gift from God and take the first few moments of each day to thank Him, we get off on the right foot! When God gets our first moments of each day we remind ourselves of His love, His protection, and commandments. We can trust Him to take care of us all of our days! If we're wise, we'll align our priorities for the coming day with the teachings and commandments that God has given us through His Holy Word.

APPENDIX A
THE F.A.I.T.H. STRATEGY

In your personal opinion, what do you understand it takes for a person to go to heaven? The Bible answers this very question and I would like to share it with you right now. You can use the word *FAITH* to get the answer.

F is for **Forgiveness**

We cannot have eternal life and heaven without God's forgiveness. *"He is so rich in kindness and grace that he purchased our freedom with the blood of his Son and forgave our sins" (Ephesians 1:7).*

A is for **Available**

Forgiveness is available. It is available for all. *"For God so loved the world that He gave His one and only Son, that whoever believes in Him shall not perish but have eternal life" (John 3:16).*

Available, but not automatic. *"Not everyone who says to me, Lord, Lord, will enter the kingdom of heaven" (Matthew 7:21).*

I is for **Impossible**

It is impossible for God to allow sin into heaven.

GOD is ...   **Love** (John 3:16).

> **Just** *"There will be no mercy for those who have not shown mercy to others. But if you have been merciful, God will be merciful when he judges you" (James 2:13).*

Man is ...   **sinful** *"For everyone has sinned; we all fall short of God's glorious standard" (Romans 3:23).*

But how can a person enter heaven, where God allows no sin?

T is for **Turn**

If you were driving down the road and someone asked you to turn, what would he or she be asking you to do? (change direction) To turn means to repent. Turn from something---sin and self. *"And you will perish, too, unless you repent of your sins and turn to God" (Luke 13:3).* Turn to someone: trust Christ!

The Bible tells us: *"I passed on to you what was most important and what had also been passed on to me. Christ died for our sins, just as the Scriptures said. He was buried, and he was raised from the dead on the third day, just as the Scriptures said." (1 Corinthians 15: 3-4).*

"If you openly declare that Jesus is Lord and believe in your heart that God raised him from the dead, you will be saved" (Romans 10:9).

H is for **Heaven**

Heaven is eternal life.

Here---*"I have come that they may have life, an abundant life" (John 10:10).*

Hereafter---*"When everything is ready, I will come and get you, so that you will always be with me where I am" (John 14:3)*

How can a person have God's forgiveness, heaven, and eternal life, and Jesus as personal Savior and Lord?

F orsaking

A ll

I

T rust

H im

"If you openly declare that Jesus is Lord and believe in your heart that God raised him from the dead, you will be saved" (Romans 10:9).

If you understand this, you can receive forgiveness by trusting in Christ as your personal Lord and Savior. Do this by praying to God and asking Him to forgive you and to save you. By doing this you become a child of God! When you're a part of God's family you have divine resources that will enable you to overcome your daily challenges! Let a Christian friend, parent, pastor, minister or teacher know of your decision! Tell the world!

LEADER'S GUIDE

APPENDIX B

UNDERSTANDING THE HIGHER POWER: A BIBLE APPLICATION STUDY ABOUT GOD

Congratulations for agreeing to facilitate this study about Understanding the Higher Power who we call God! Your influence and guidance will reap eternal benefits to men, women, and young people who will be ambassadors for Christ. Enjoy yourself through this journey and expect to be blessed beyond measure because that's the way God works!

Here are a few preparations to complete before you begin the study.

1) Publicize, "Understanding the Higher Power" about four weeks before the first session is scheduled. Although the study is written primarily for adults, a maturing teenager could benefit from it. Use it as an outreach opportunity. It's written for all types of backgrounds.

2) Order books for all participants. Learners will use their own personal copies of the books, taking them home for interactive study. At the end of the study, they'll use them for future reference.

3) Decide on the length of each session. For each weekly discussion session, 45 minutes to an hour is most sufficient. Extra time for fellowship and prayer should be considered.

4) Decide on the size of you group. If it's a small group you may want to meet together. If it's a medium to large group, you may want to select small group leaders to allow for more intimate, personal discussions.

5) If you are leading the session, complete all chapters yourself, along with the learner, so that you can easily facilitate discussions.

6) Pray for each learner who will join your study. Ask God to prepare their heart, as well as yours.

DURING THE FIRST SESSION

The first session with your learners will set the tone for the rest of the study. Try to make the environment as comfortable, safe, and friendly and fun as possible. Playing Christian music in the background as learners arrive is always a good idea. Serving refreshments is always optional and may be a good idea. Chairs formed in a circle are great for open discussion and small groups. If a table is needed for the written portion or note taking then don't hesitate to use one. Young people may find it comfortable to just sit on the floor! Whatever you decide, remember your enthusiasm and personal genuineness in greeting them will make for a positive first impression.

1) Greet learners warmly. Consider nametags if you expect visitors to be present and consider using an "icebreaker". Introduce yourself and share a little about your passion for teaching this study.

2) Pass around a contact sheet so students can write their names, addresses, phone numbers, and e-mail addresses. Keep this sheet for your personal records for future outreach and encouragement.

3) Distribute "Understanding the Higher Power", asking each learner to write their name inside the front cover. Explain that this is their personal copy to take home, to write in, and to bring each

week to the Bible study.

4) Introduce the Bible study by asking learners to share a question about God they've struggled with. Write their responses on a chalkboard, dry erase board, or poster paper so that everyone can see. Use the list as a spring board for several discussion questions:

- Say, "Which item on the list is particularly confusing to you?" Ask for a show of hands for each item listed.

- Say, "Why is _____ so hard to understand?" (choose an item on the list).

5. Ask the learners to open their books to the Table of Contents and glance at specific topics for the next eight weeks. Point out any items on their "Hardship" list that appear in the Table of Contents. Ask learners which week/topic that they look forward to discussing most.

6. Turn to Week 1/First Chapter page, "This Is God's World"

- Ask learners to read the first paragraph silently and then to answer the question: "Is there something about creation and nature that turns your mind to God?" Discuss their responses.

- Read Psalm 24:1 (verse is provided in the space

after the chapter title). Answer the first set of "Questions to Consider" aloud with students, giving them time to write their answers.

- Ask, "Did you know that every living creature is dependent on God?" Wait for answers. Then have someone read Psalm 104"27-30 in their Bible. Talk about time and the process of taking care of pets and animals. Then direct them to the second set of "Questions to Consider" and ask: "What do you feel about those who believe that evolution is the process God used to create human?" Use Scripture (Genesis 1:26 and others) to discuss the question.

- Read aloud the last paragraph of the chapter found in the "Follow-Up", so the students know they have home study to complete before the next session.

- Ask for prayer requests. If someone is comfortable praying aloud, then let them volunteer. If not, then everyone may pray silently or you may close the session in prayer.

FOR THE REMAINING SESSIONS

The purpose of each weekly session is to discuss specific topics in depth, facilitating questions and giving students a chance to learn from each other (and from you). These suggestions will keep each session's format fresh and exciting:

1) Facilitate each weeks session by opening up with a brief prayer thanking God for this time to study and for clarity of mind to understand the material covered. Read the opening Scripture, objectives of the chapter and the central truth. Let the learners complete some of the "Questions to Consider" on their own. But always refer to Scriptures during the discussion so that any advice or instructions is based on God's truth alone.

2) You may want to begin the session by asking learners which parts of the sessions were particularly meaningful for them, and start the discussion from there. Be flexible, knowing that a lengthy discussion on one topic can be as important as short discussions covering all the sessions material.

3) After a few weeks, you may ask for learner volunteers to lead discussions on particular questions for the following week. Learners probably need specific instructions (assign a set of :Questions to Consider" and have them share their responses first and they can ask for comments from others). By the end of the study, you may be able to assign future "Questions to Consider" for the nest week's session. Realize, of course, that you'll need to supplement or gently

re-direct the discussion when necessary.

4) Look for stories from newspapers and magazine articles that might relate to the topics discussed. Perhaps you can show a video clip of another relating matter. Always search for current events and resources that you can use while leading the sessions.

5) Feel free to bring in guest speakers to share briefly on the session topics. Just be sure the speaker leaves time for learners to discuss their thoughts.

6) Never underestimate the value of personal stories and experiences you can share with the learners. This helps the learners comprehend your empathy. Obviously, choose appropriate stories that are brief and relatable to their experiences.

7) Take time each week for prayer requests and encourage and praise learners for things they're learning and accomplishing in their lives. You might also provide index cards for students to write private prayer concerns for your eyes only.

TIPS FOR A SUCCESSFUL STUDY

1) Encourage students to complete all eight sessions. Moreover, stress the importance of pacing themselves with the completion of one session/one chapter per week. Understanding the Higher

Power takes more than a lifetime and it takes time to adequately digest the Scriptures and revelations.

2) Realize that some learners may not be Christians because they haven't yet placed their faith in Jesus Christ. At some point in the study, at least as a review at the end, discuss the F.A.I.T.H. method presented in the appendix of the study book. Take as long as needed to explain Salvation. Some follow-up with learners can be expected even after the study is completed.

3) Tell the learners that you're praying for them by name every day. Then do it!

4) Never allow a learner to degrade or put down another learner because of some past experience that's shared or insinuated.

5) Assure learners that each weekly session is a safe place to ask questions, vent frustrations, or reveal problems. Make an effort to speak with each learner every week if at all possible. Encourage learners that you welcome private prayer concerns and that you will gladly pray with them. Occasionally write your learners a short note and mail it, send an e-mail, or give them a phone call. People like this!

Look forward to spending time with your learners.

They're hungry for godly people who show interest in them and answers to questions they have about the Higher Power, otherwise they would not come to the sessions. They will love you, and you'll love them too.

NOTES
THIS IS GOD'S WORLD

NOTES
OUR REBELLION AGAINST GOD

NOTES
GOD'S CONCERN FOR ME

NOTES
GOD LOVES YOU, REGARDLESS

NOTES
GOD WORKS THROUGH ME

GOD SPEAKS TO ME
THROUGH CHRIST

GOD'S POWER WILL
SUSTAIN ME TO THE END

THE PRIORITY OF GOD
IN MY LIFE

NOTES
APPENDIX

AUTHOR

Can be found on Amazon, Barnes & Noble, and other book distributors in the United States.